Mastering™

Red Hat™ Linux 9

Michael Jang

San Francisco   London

Associate Publisher: Joel Fugazzotto

Acquisitions Editor: Ellen L. Dendy

Developmental Editor: Brianne Agatep

Production Editor: Leslie E.H. Light

Technical Editor: Elizabeth Zinkann

Copyeditor: Liz Welch

Compositors: Jill Niles and Maureen Forys

Graphic Illustrator: Jeffrey Wilson, Happenstance Type-o-Rama

CD Coordinator: Dan Mummert

Proofreaders: Emily Hsuan, Nancy Riddiough, Susanne Stein, Laura Schattshneider, Eric Lack

Indexer: Ted Laux

Book Designer: Maureen Forys, Happenstance Type-o-Rama

Cover Designer: Design Site

Cover Photographer: Sergie Loobkoff

Library of Congress Card Number: 2003100048
ISBN: 0-7821-4179-X

Software License Agreement

To the young widows and widowers everywhere: our lives will never be the same. But life can be good again.

My dear Nancy, I miss you. I feel joy as your spirit lives on through me. I'm doing the good things you've always encouraged me to do. I am determined to live well for the both of us.

Acknowledgments

IT ALMOST TAKES A village to create a computer book. Ellen Dendy had the foresight to propose this book, in time for the Linux-led renaissance of the tech sector. Brianne Agatep has guided the development of this book from start to finish, marvelously making sure it stayed on track. Leslie Light's excellent production management skills helped me focus on my writing during this difficult personal time. Liz Welch's editing skills have helped make this book readable by anyone interested in Linux.

This book could not go to press without the dedication and hard work of the other members of the team, including Jill Niles, Maureen Forys, Ted Laux, and Elizabeth Campbell.

Most importantly to this book, and to finding new life, I give special thanks to Elizabeth Zinkann, technical editor extraordinaire, logical Linux catalyst, and great friend. Not only is she the most Linux-savvy technical editor that I've ever encountered, she's been there to listen and help as I've worked through my grief.

It does take a community to raise an operating system. I thank the thousands of developers around the world who donate their time to building Linux into an operating system that is challenging a monopoly. Two of them helped me work through some of the newer graphical applications for this book: Rob Buis of the KDE project and Jody Goldberg of the GNOME project.

On a personal note, thank you, Donna. Thank you for your love and support. Thank you for helping me to understand that we will always miss our dearly departed mates. Thank you for inspiring me to find life and love again. You are the love of my new life. Thank you for the new memories we are building together.

I hope; therefore I can live.

Contents at a Glance